Complete Guide to

Anonymous Torrent Downloading & File-sharing

Matthew Bailey

A practical, step-by-step guide on how to protect your Internet privacy and anonymity both online and offline while torrenting

www.cogipas.com

Table of Contents

PART I – ABOUT TORRENTS, THE RISKS, AND WHAT YOU'LL NEED TO BE ANONYMOUS

Introduction

This Guide has been written with everyone in mind. It starts with the assumption that you know nothing about torrents and are approaching this Guide with little more at your disposal than an Internet connection and a suitable device (whether a desktop computer, laptop, tablet or smart phone). Starting from this humble base, I will explain each and every step of the anonymous torrent downloading process. If you are more advanced in your knowledge of torrents, merely jump to the part of this Guide that is best suited to your needs.

Top Tip - Throughout this Guide, I'll use the generic term *device* to mean the desktop computer, laptop, tablet or smart phone you are using, whether it operates on Windows, Mac OS, Linux, iOS or Android. I'll also use *apps* to mean applications and software that run on devices.

What are Torrents?

BitTorrents (I'll use just *torrents* for short in this Guide) were developed in 2001 (yep, more than a decade ago!) but their importance and popularity as a means of file-sharing on the Internet continue to grow.

Torrents are small text files that contain just a few pieces of information on how its particular *payload* can be downloaded over a network. Put another way, a torrent file provides a means of where and how to download a torrent's payload.

A torrent's payload is a collection of one or more digital items ranging from full-length movies, music files, video clips, ebooks, documents, apps, software programs, images, documents to basically any digital content that you can think of.

For example, a torrent's payload could be a single item, such as an individual music file, or it could be a set of similar items like a collection of music files, numbering upwards of dozens to hundreds. But a torrent's payload could also comprise any number of and different types of items, such as a full-length movie bundled together with a subtitles text file, soundtrack mp3 music file, a movie-themed game app and images from a behind-the-scenes photo shoot, all associated with one torrent.

You download and share torrents with their own special kind of app, a *torrent app*. Even though torrents themselves are just small text files their payloads can be massive because the torrents do not actually *contain* the payload items; instead, the torrents merely *enable* your torrent app to locate and download the payload items on the torrent network.

Furthermore, you can download a single torrent or have many torrents working at the same time. Needless to say, there is a wealth of torrents out there waiting for you to download and share, whether you are interested in movies, music, apps, video clips, games, books, erotica, images, or whole collections of these items. For example, if you find the right torrent you can download dozens or hundreds of items in one go or cherry-pick among the individual items associated with the torrent. This is the great thing about the torrent format.

The collective group of people downloading and sharing a torrent at any one time on the torrent network is called a *swarm*. When you open a torrent, it informs your torrent app how to download the payload items from the torrent's swarm on the network. Of course, a swarm is always changing as more or fewer people share a specific torrent.

Top Tip - If torrents are a new concept to you, don't worry. Although torrents and how to download them can seem a little complicated to the newcomer, once you get to understand the basic concepts, you will soon get the hang of them and be able to enjoy the many torrent downloads on offer. And anonymously too! How to find torrents and use a torrent app are all explained in the pages ahead.

Torrent files usually end in the extension .torrent (*download-me.torrent*). The information in the small torrent files is used by torrent apps to find pieces of the payload items shared among an entire swarm. The bigger the swarm (the more people sharing the torrent), the faster you can download its payload.

Torrents and their payloads can be downloaded in a few easy steps, but doing so *anonymously* means taking a few extra steps in the process. However, the extra steps are not difficult and are well worth the effort.

By definition, any kind of file-sharing over the Internet, including downloading torrents, means sharing your device's *IP address*, your unique online digital fingerprint. As a result, the extra steps needed to download torrents anonymously include protecting your IP address from disclosure so that people cannot snoop on your torrent activities. As downloading torrents will leave certain information behind on your device, the extra steps also include ways of cleansing away these traces. Thankfully, the extra steps you can take to counter these online and offline risks are relatively easy. These steps are all described in detail later in this Guide.

How Torrents Work

In contrast to downloading from the web, torrent payloads are not downloaded from any one place. Instead they are downloaded from many other users, like you, who are online and sharing the same torrent.

A torrent network connects people who are downloading and sharing torrents. People sharing the same torrent form a swarm and their torrent apps will exchange data until the torrent's payload is downloaded by all members of the swarm. Once a particular member of the swarm has downloaded a torrent's payload, the torrent continues to be shared for the benefit of the other members of the swarm.

This matching and swarming is all done seamlessly in the background by your torrent app and with the help of some servers on the Internet known as torrent *trackers* (see the *Top Tip* below). All you need to do is find the torrents you want, download them (remember they are just small text files), open them in your torrent app, and then wait for your app to download the associated payloads. The more people that are sharing the particular torrent, the faster you will be able to download them. This is why you can often download popular torrents very quickly because their swarms are large.

Top Tip - The *trackers* mentioned above are servers on the Internet that coordinate the exchanges of data going on between users sharing torrents on the torrent network.

The transfer of data on the torrent network is actually very sophisticated because the network will match people based on the smallest chunks of information available. This means that as you *download* a torrent, you are actually simultaneously *uploading* it too, sharing your partially downloaded items with the swarm on the torrent network. As soon as they can be, even the smallest parts of an item are shared with other members of the swarm.

Each member of the swarm sharing a torrent is known as a *peer*. Peers sharing a fully downloaded torrent are called *seeders*. Peers sharing a partially downloaded (incomplete) torrent are called *leechers*. If you are downloading a torrent, you are also automatically sharing it as a leecher. The more seeders a torrent has, the faster it should download. If a torrent has no seeders and too few leechers, it is possible that you may not be able to download the torrent in full. This can happen when the collective swarm does not possess a full torrent between them. Of course, at any one time seeders and leechers come and go in a swarm as its members stop sharing the torrent, go offline or close their torrent app.

This was a brief and simplified explanation of how torrents work. If you want to learn more, here is a good 3-minute video overview http://www.cogipas.com/intro-to-torrents-video. Also, this visualization is a cool way to interactively see how torrent downloading works with peers and seeds, http://www.cogipas.com/intro-to-torrents-visual.

Top Tip - When you see URLs (website addresses) in this Guide starting with www.cogipas.com/ or goo.gl/, they are just ways to make long URLs more manageable by shortening them. The first address is via my own website, while the second is via Google.

How to Download Torrents

The technical aspects behind how torrents work are fascinating. But let's now turn to how it works in practice.

Just as you use a web browsing app for browsing the web or a word processing app for opening documents, you will need a torrent app for downloading torrents.

When you find a torrent file that you want to download (don't worry, I'll soon tell you everything you need to know about finding torrents), you click on it just as you would for downloading a document from a website. Upon clicking on the link, your web browser will prompt you to download the torrent file. This is the same process as when clicking on a document online.

As it is just a tiny text file, the torrent will download very quickly to your device. To open the torrent, you would just click on it. Again, this is exactly the same process as when you successfully download a document from the web and then want to open it.

Now here is where things get a little different. When your torrent app opens the torrent that you just downloaded, you will be presented with some information and prompted to make some choices. Your torrent app will display information about the torrent you just downloaded, usually its name and the payload items associated with the torrent. The payload could be a single item or could number in the dozens of items. Again, don't make the mistake of thinking that the payload items are actually *inside* the torrent file you just downloaded (in contrast to a ZIP file for example), because they aren't.

You can also make some choices before you start downloading the torrent's payload. Depending on the torrent app, you can select which of the payload items to download. This means that you can skip certain items, if you wish. For example, perhaps the torrent you downloaded is associated with a payload of 10 music files and you only want one of them. You can just download the one item you want and skip the rest, not wasting any time or extra bandwidth on the other items.

Depending on the torrent app and the device (for example, computer versus a smartphone) you may also be prompted for *where* on the device to save the payload items.

Once you have finished making your choices, you can start the payload downloading process. Usually this happens when you click OK after making your choices.

Your torrent app will now show the torrent as an *active* torrent. This means that your torrent app (with the help of the trackers I talked about a few pages earlier) is looking to join the swarm and start communicating with other peers and begin the payload downloading process. As mentioned, depending on the torrent's popularity, you may quickly join a swarm and start downloading almost immediately or it might take hours, days or even weeks in the case of obscure torrents.

Your torrent app will display which torrents are active and the progress of your downloads. Once a torrent's payload is 100% downloaded (or the subset of items that you selected from the available payload) your torrent app will show that you are now *seeding* the torrent. Once a torrent's payload is completely downloaded you can stop sharing the torrent, but good torrent etiquette dictates that you do some sharing too. After all, if no one seeded torrents, payloads would be much more difficult and slow to download.

And that's it! The payload items will now be saved to your device for you to enjoy.

This was just an overview. In Part II, I go through the process in step-by-step detail, including some screenshots and recommendations.

The Privacy Risks of Downloading Torrents

There are both online and offline risks from downloading torrents. Let's briefly look at these risks.

Online Risks

Downloading and sharing torrents can *feel* anonymous, but this is deceptive. Like all Internet communications, torrent activities inevitably involve the interaction of IP addresses. In order for everyone in the swarm to be able to connect to one another, this involves the interaction of IP addresses (everyone's devices need to share IP addresses to exchange data).

IP addresses are the online digital fingerprints assigned to and used by devices on the Internet to connect to one another. Your IP address is "stamped" on all of your Internet activities, whether browsing web pages, sending emails, exchanging chat messages, downloading apps, posting to social networks, etc. Your IP address is also stamped on all your torrent downloading and sharing activities.

If you do not take steps to hide your IP address, your torrent downloading activities can be easily ascertained. OK, so what?

If a snoop wants to determine your IP address, he just needs to share a torrent to join its swarm and then monitor the activities. However, if you use a *torrent anonymizing service* (discussed soon) the users with whom you connect in the swarm will only see data transfers to and from a *masked* IP address assigned by your anonymizing service rather than your true IP address. This way, the anonymizing service acts as an intermediary standing between you and the prying eyes of any snoops.

In addition, many Internet service providers (ISPs) frown on their customers using torrents because of the potentially large amounts of data involved. If your ISP detects that you are downloading torrents, they may throttle (slow down) your connection. There are also aggressive firms monitoring torrent activities and in some cases threatening users with payment demands or legal action. Another factor is that some people may be downloading torrents about subjects that they would rather keep private, such as relating to health or medical conditions, financial matters or other private information that is nobody else's business. Other people may want to keep their online activities private purely out of principle, for example, in reaction to increasing intrusion and overreach on the part of businesses or governments.

As you can see, wanting to keep your torrent downloading habits under the radar does *not* mean that you have something to hide. Not at all. Whatever your reasons for wanting to keep your torrent activities private and as anonymous as possible, the steps in this Guide apply.

To see an example of how torrent downloaders are being monitored, see http://www.cogipas.com/torrent-monitoring/.

Offline Risks

Even though these are more secondary in nature, there are also offline privacy risks from downloading torrents. Even if you manage to download torrents privately and anonymously, thereby preventing detection by online snoops, you should still take some steps to ensure that anyone who has or can gain access to your device is prevented from discovering your private material.

The steps for doing this are not difficult, but too few people implement them. For completeness, in this Guide I will also cover the steps you can take to prevent the offline risks from downloading torrents.

Copyright Infringement

Speaking of risks, let me just come right out and say it: a lot of torrents are pirated. That's a pity. Piracy undercuts the efforts of the very content producers you enjoy. While it may not always be easy to tell which torrents are associated with pirated copyright materials, you usually know it when you see it. A bit like with spam for email, the more you use torrents, the better you will be at spotting the torrents to avoid.

Torrent file-sharing technology is itself legal, but some or even many of the payloads being shared on torrent networks are pirated copyright material. Downloading pirated copyright material, *even by accident*, can get you in trouble. Torrents do not have to be synonymous with copyright infringement, so use the technology responsibly and legally.

You should respect copyright and by doing so support the content producers of the materials you enjoy. If we support pirated materials – whether by not paying for them or otherwise failing to honor the copyright owner's terms – the materials could stop being made.

Following this advice will also help you stay out of potential trouble with those elements that are tirelessly trying to make copyright offenders pay should you inadvertently download copyright materials (hey, it can happen to anyone). Breaching copyright, whether intentionally or accidentally, can have consequences. These consequences can include your ISP cutting off your service, industry associations dragging you into lawsuits or lawyers sending letters on behalf of copyright clients demanding monetary compensation.

While it is true that following the techniques in this Guide will maximize the anonymity of your torrent activities and make it difficult for anyone to discover your torrent habits, it is safest to steer clear of the pirated stuff and respect copyright.

Malware-Infected and Fake Torrents

While some torrents infringe copyright, others are infected with malware, so caution is warranted. In particular, you should use a malware app to rigorously scan all items that you have downloaded via torrents before opening them.

Top Tip - Many excellent free malware apps are available, including MalwareBytes Anti-malware (free) at http://www.malwarebytes.org/ for Windows, Avast Free Antivirus (free) at http://www.avast.com/ for Mac OS and Linux, and AVG Antivirus (free) at http://www.avg.com/eu-en/antivirus-for-android for Android devices.

In addition, some torrents are fake. When you download a fake torrent the payload does not turn out to be what you expected. Fake torrents can occur by accident (when the torrent was being created) but usually fake torrents are created intentionally as a form of mischief. While fake torrents do not pose the same kind of danger as the malware infected ones, they result in you wasting time, effort and bandwidth.

What You Will Need

For now, I quickly list the apps and services that you will need to download and share torrents. Should you wish to get the apps now, the links are provided. This is just *what* you will need. *How* you use the apps and services outlined below will be set out in detailed steps in Part II of the Guide.

In addition, a summary of all the apps and services I recommend appear in a handy Annex (Quick Start Resources) towards the end of this Guide.

A Torrent App

First, you will need a torrent app. As already discussed, a torrent app is used to open torrents and download their payloads to your device.

A good choice is µTorrent (free) at http://www.utorrent.com/ for Windows and Mac OS. There is also a beta version of µTorrent for Android (free) via http://goo.gl/41X1lg or http://www.utorrent.com/utorrent-android which has a handy WiFi mode which lets you choose to download and seed only when connected to WiFi, cutting down on mobile connection charges.

Please note that it is called "microtorrent", not "you torrent". µTorrent is small, fast and has tens of *millions* of active users every month, which helps to ensure that there are lots of people for you to share torrents with. The free version does display ads, but they are unobtrusive and can actually be used to your advantage (explained a bit later). It also has a handy "boss key" for quickly hiding the app should an unwelcome visitor drop by unexpectedly.

If you prefer, you can use any torrent-compatible app that you want. Another popular choice of torrent app is *Vuze* (free) at http://www.vuze.com/ for Windows, Mac OS and Linux. Or *Transmission* (free) at http://www.transmissionbt.com/ for Mac OS. For iOS, Apple's App Store doesn't carry torrent apps so you'll have to use an intermediary service like *zbigz* at http://zbigz.com/.

An IP Address Protection Tool

Although it is not mandatory that you use an IP address protection tool while downloading torrents, these tools help prevent "unfriendly" IP addresses from connecting with your device.

For Windows, I recommend *PeerBlock* (free) at http://www.peerblock.com/.

For Mac OS, PeerGuardian (free) works on a similar concept, but is now outdated. Mac users are better off relying on the IP protection feature built-in to the Mac torrent app mentioned above, *Transmission*.

A Torrent Anonymizing Service

As mentioned, the key to maximizing your privacy and anonymity when downloading torrents is to protect your IP address from disclosure. While an IP address protection tool helps *shield* your IP address from potential torrent snoops, the best protection is to *hide* your IP address outright. This way, even if your IP address is detected while you are downloading torrents, it is not your "real" IP address and you remain safe. After all, the IP address protection tool, though helpful, cannot be expected to block 100% of potentially unfriendly elements that may be trying to snoop on you.

The best way to hide your IP address is to use a specialized *torrent anonymizing service*. These services will hide your IP address *and* encrypt your traffic, protecting your torrent activities from being snooped on whether by your ISP wanting to throttle your bandwidth or from outside parties eavesdropping on your connection and monitoring your downloads.

With a torrent anonymizing service enabled:

1) your ISP will only see encrypted (scrambled) traffic. They can still see *how much* data you are downloading, but not *what* it is or even that it is

torrent traffic (though it may not be that hard for them to guess if you are downloading high data volumes).

2) outside snoops will not be able to eavesdrop on or monitor your torrent activities as they will be unable to attribute the data traffic to your true IP address. Every time you connect to the torrent anonymizing service your torrent traffic will be tunneled through, and seem to be coming from, a different IP address.

Using an anonymizing service to hide your true IP address and scramble your torrent traffic makes it very difficult for snoops to monitor you. While nothing can 100% guarantee your full anonymity, the privacy advantages of using these services when downloading and sharing torrents should now be obvious.

Although using an anonymizing service may sound intimidating, many of these services now take the techno complexity out of them and are easy to use. After opening an account with the torrent anonymizing service provider, it is usually as simple as downloading a small app or piece of software and entering your credentials (username and password). You will be downloading torrents anonymously in no time. It really can be that simple.

Free vs. Premium Services
Unfortunately, the reality is that there is no free lunch when it comes to these services. Some free options do exist, but they are usually less convenient and suffer from slower download speeds.

If you perform some easy Internet searches, you will quickly find plenty of free anonymizing services. However, few if any of them support *torrents*. This is due to the high downloading volumes associated with torrent activities. Even if you find a free service that does support torrents, there is always going to be a catch. Sometimes configuring them is difficult, especially for less knowledgeable users, increasing the chances of getting things wrong. Or the "free" service somehow makes *you* the product, for example, by injecting annoying ads into your experience or mining your personal data and preferences. Plus, any free torrent anonymizing service can be expected to have a weaker *privacy policy* when compared to paid services. With any free service, you would have to be especially trusting as, remember, you will be routing your torrent activities through them.

The most convenient and fastest services supporting torrents are "premium" in nature and do cost money. Thankfully, the costs are relatively low and seem to be dropping all the time. I realize it is a personal choice, but I would say that it is worth spending a little money to get a reliable and trustworthy premium service. Most will not cost you more per month than a couple of coffees at your local coffee shop.

Of course, the desire to spend a little money will also depend on how much you value keeping your torrent downloading activities private. If it's not that important to you, use a free service. If it is important to keep your torrent downloading activities private, consider paying a little for a premium service.

Let me clarify something right away: you might think that the most widely known of these free services is TOR, also known as the TOR Project or the Onion Router. It is true that TOR is a free and widely known web anonymizing service. Did you catch that? *Web* anonymizing, not *torrent* anonymizing. TOR is *completely* inappropriate for torrents. TOR's own materials make this clear, https://blog.torproject.org/blog/bittorrent-over-tor-isnt-good-idea. The post is dated 2010, but the point is still valid: TOR is not a suitable torrent anonymizing solution.

WARNING!

As just mentioned, you need a *torrent* anonymizing service. While there are a number of free *web* anonymizing services (TOR being the most widely-known but there are countless others such as Hotspot Shield) these web anonymizing services will *not* work with torrents. Torrents and web browsing use different *protocols* or ways of communicating on the Internet. Web anonymizing services work with the *http/https* protocol used for web browsing, but not with the *peer-to-peer* (*p2p* for short) protocol used for torrents. You will see this illustrated in detail soon when I discuss Step 3 about making sure that your torrent anonymizing service is working and hiding your true IP address. This critical difference between the two protocols and the anonymizing services associated with them is also why this Guide expressly distinguishes between *web* and *torrent* anonymizing services. It's an important difference, so keep it in mind.

Adding to the potential confusion is that sometimes the claims made by web anonymizing services are vague enough to make you think that they will also work for torrents. If you do not see "works for downloading torrents" expressly listed as part of the service's features, it probably does *not* work for torrents. You can always directly ask the service, but be skeptical about any claims that are not backed up. Do your research.

Unfortunately, at the time of writing I am not aware of any reliable free *torrent* anonymizing services that I can recommend. If you discover any, please share them with everyone in the comments section of the page http://www.cogipas.com/free-anonymizing-torrent-services.

The same warning above regarding free services also applies to the premium services. Make sure that any premium service you consider using expressly states among its features that it works for torrents. If the premium service you are considering has a "try before you buy" offer, use this and perform the upcoming verification Step 3 before signing up.

What service to choose is probably the most important decision you will make in achieving maximum torrent privacy and anonymity. For these reasons, in the upcoming Detailed Steps discussion in Part II, I provide a number of strategies and suggestions for you to consider when making your choice. After showing you how to make the best choice, I also provide some recommendations for your consideration.

Encryption and Washing-Up Apps

These sorts of tools are *optional* in so far as they are about protecting you from the *offline* risks of downloading and sharing torrents. As mentioned, in addition to protecting your torrent activities from being detected *online*, you may want to protect the disclosure of your torrent downloads from anyone that has or gains access to your device.

Not to sound paranoid, but there are plenty of stories about someone's downloads being used against them whether by a jilted lover, private investigator, divorce attorney, rogue co-worker, business rival, nosy neighbor, hacker, troll, or even Big Brother. Regardless, it's never fun having your private material discovered, whether accidentally by those who have access to your devices, or intentionally by determined adversaries, such as some of those just mentioned.

Encryption

Unfortunately, encryption is a term that scares many people off. That is a shame. If you are comfortable inserting a USB stick and seeing a new drive letter appear on your laptop or desktop computer to which you then save, copy and delete items, today's encryption apps work as simple as that.

You can use an encryption app to encrypt (secure) individual items (whether torrents or their payloads), entire folders (including all the items contained in the folder) or even your entire device (including its operating system and apps) for ultimate protection.

Using an encryption app is like having the combination to an impenetrable safe that only you can open. To anyone who does not possess the correct password you set, the items you selected for encryption - whether on your device, USB sticks, external hard drives or in the cloud - will be totally inaccessible. Upon entering your password, the items appear as if by magic with no loss of time or storage space. It really couldn't be easier and *everyone* should be using encryption, especially for torrents.

One of the best encryption apps is also completely free, TrueCrypt (free) at http://www.truecrypt.org/ for Windows, Mac OS and Linux. In addition, its online documentation and tutorials are excellent.

Other encryption apps include *SSE-Universal Encryption App* (free) via http://goo.gl/o6UmeO for Android, *Encryption Buddy* (premium) via http://goo.gl/w3TsVa for Mac OS, *Safe* (premium) at http://goo.gl/ZiDljj for iOS, and *Folder Lock* (premium after free trial period) at http://www.newsoftwares.net/folderlock/ for Windows.

Of course, the protection offered by encryption apps is only as strong as the passwords you use. Therefore, use a long password (a pass *phrase* is actually better) with a mix of uppercase and lowercase letters, numbers and even symbols.

Washing-Up

A washing-up app removes the traces of the most recent activities from your device. Like the cleaning crew after a party, a washing-up app clears your device of the clutter and trash left behind after a session of downloading torrents. Put plainly, a washing-up app will clear your device of the *traces* of torrents that may appear in places such as your trash or recycle bin, or the history lists kept by your device and its apps about the items you most recently accessed, whether with movie players, image viewers, document readers or music players.

A good free app is *CCleaner* (free) at http://www.piriform.com/ccleaner for Windows and Mac OS. For Android devices, check out *Clean Master* (free) via http://goo.gl/UrNgbX. For iOS, try *iCleaner* (premium) via http://goo.gl/y6q5UF.

For Windows, I can also recommend *Privacy Eraser Pro* (premium ¢) via http://www.cogipas.com/pep. It comes with a trial evaluation period, supports all major web browsers, and includes access to hundreds of plug-ins available for almost every app imaginable; some that you probably didn't even know were keeping records of your activities. As an added bonus, it comes with a built-in file wiping utility for permanently deleting items on your device (acting like an electronic shredder).

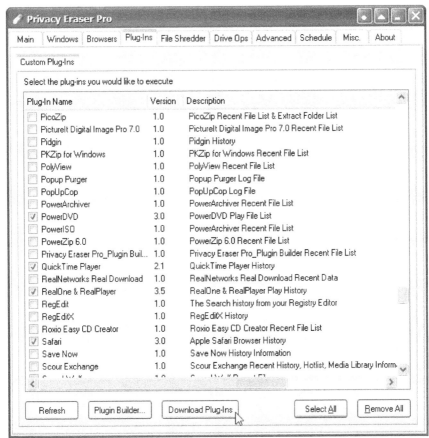

Figure 1: Privacy Eraser Pro lets you customize the items to wash-up from your device

Outro

Phew! Now that I've outlined *what* you'll need and in general *why*, let's move on to the detailed steps of *how*. But first, as promised, I will provide some suggestions on the all-important topic of how to choose a torrent anonymizing service that's right for you. I'll also provide some of my own recommendations, in case you find that helpful.

Then we get into the nitty-gritty steps of exactly how to go about downloading torrents as privately and anonymously as possible. Of course, this process also includes how to *find* torrents to download and enjoy in the first place. I'll cover all of this and more in the pages ahead.

Choosing a Torrent Anonymizing Service

A few pages back I outlined that, unfortunately, *free* torrent anonymizing services are hard to come by. Even if you do find a potentially suitable free service, please keep in mind that free services can be expected to have weaker privacy protections, engage in logging, serve ads or track your activities. This section assumes that you want to explore the option of a suitable *premium* (paid) torrent anonymizing service.

Of course, any reliance on a third party acting as a shield in the middle of the torrent downloading process requires a high degree of trust on your part. For example, services purporting to offer anonymity state that they are not keeping activity logs that can be used to link user activity. But who can say for sure? You should only use reliable and time-tested services, but this is not always easy to determine.

Emotions run high when talking about which anonymizing service is the "best". But remember, this depends on lots of factors and everyone's situation is different. The following are some factors for you to consider.

Cost

The price each service charges is an obvious factor in your choice and a very personal one. Some people can afford or are willing to spend more, others are not. However, as many of the services are similarly priced - on average, usually about $5-10 per month (about £3-7 or €4-8) depending on the length of the contract you choose - the decision often comes down to features and reliability. That said, these services sometimes have time-limited promotions and usually offer discounts for longer contract periods, so keep an eye out for deals.

Although different from cost, perhaps payment options are important to you. Some people are not comfortable paying by credit card and want to see PayPal or other payment options, like BitCoin.

Before signing up to a longer-term plan, start with a short-term one first to make sure that everything works well for you. Many services offer 3-day, weekly or monthly plans. Some even offer free trials or money-back guarantees.

Supports Torrents (p2p)

For features, the most important thing is to make sure that the service supports torrents. As mentioned, look for specific statements in the service's offering and documentation. (Although you are less likely to see mention of the "peer-to-peer (p2p) protocol", this means the same thing). However, this is not always easy as many anonymizing services don't expressly advertise the fact that they support torrents.

Your base requirement is that the service hides your true IP address when you are downloading and sharing torrents, and that it encrypts your torrent traffic.

Torrent anonymizing services may also offer some advanced features, such as allowing you to choose the location of the *exit gateways* (the countries in which the service's proxy servers are located). This gives you some control over which country the IP address your torrent traffic will seem to be coming from. So, if you live in the US, this kind of feature would let you pick exit gateways located in, for example, Canada or Sweden. Anyone snooping on your torrent traffic will think it is coming to and from Canada or Sweden, rather than the US. If the snoop traced back the traffic to the proxy servers located in Sweden, this would lead them to the torrent anonymizing service, rather than you. To make sure that the chain of discovery will end at your service provider and not be further traced back to you, see the upcoming *Private Policy* section. Generally speaking, you want a service that has exit gateways in many different locations, the more the better.

Other features offered by torrent anonymizing services might include allowing you to *automatically* select the fastest exit gateways at any given time. Yet other features will even let you "split" your connection so that the Internet traffic for some apps, like torrents, are routed through the service and anonymized, while the traffic for your other apps continue to be routed through a regular (non-anonymized) Internet connection.

Top Tip - There may be times when you do *not* want to anonymize some of your Internet traffic through foreign exit gateways, particularly when web browsing, because many websites, such as search engines or online retailers, automatically redirect you to their country-specific sites or restrict the content you can stream or access.

Many torrent anonymizing services are full-fledged *VPNs*, virtual private networks. VPN services hide your true IP address by routing *all* of your Internet traffic, including your torrent traffic, through a different network of servers they maintain, thereby acting as a proxy between your device and the rest of the Internet. This means that using a VPN as your torrent anonymizing service also provides you with the "bonus" of being able to also use it to hide your IP address for all your other online activities too, including web browsing.

Again, it's not that you have anything to hide, but using a VPN for your other Internet activities can, for example, make you less susceptible to the online tracking and profiling in which advertisers and other businesses engage. It can also help protect you from snoops who try to monitor torrent activities by cross-referencing your other Internet activities like web browsing, a technique called *traffic analysis*. I will provide an example of this a little later.

Top Tip - Further references in this Guide to VPNs mean anonymizing services that anonymize *all* of your Internet traffic thereby acting as *both* a torrent anonymizing service *and* a web anonymizing service.

A Word about Technical Specifications

Sometimes you will see a long list of various technical specifications itemized among a service's features, especially VPNs. These technical terms may include PPTP, L2TP IPSec, SSTP, OpenVPN, SSL, TLS. Don't let these confuse you. The bottom line is that they all provide a secure, encrypted connection keeping your activities safe from eavesdropping and monitoring, whether from your ISP or from other potential snoops.

So you do not need to get wrapped up in what these are. You also don't need to worry about which one of the technical specifications is "best". Each one has its intricacies, but not enough for us to worry about when downloading and sharing torrents. What we need is something that provides a secure (encrypted) connection and hides our true IP address, masking it with a decoy one.

Top Tip - Please keep in mind that, though these services anonymize your traffic and help ensure your online privacy, they do not make you invincible to things like viruses, malware and other similar threats. So keep practicing good habits on your devices, such as using anti-malware apps and being careful about the attachments and links you open.

Customer Experience

Customer experience, in particular for torrent users, should also be a factor that weighs on your choice of torrent anonymizing service. While the service provider's website will tout lots of satisfied customers and testimonials (what else would you expect?), some research is in order.

To determine customers' experiences, check long-standing, reliable third party sources of information about the service(s) you are considering. One of the most trusted sources of up-to-date information in the torrent community is TorrentFreak at http://torrentfreak.com/.

You can also Google around to find information about customers' experiences. However, make sure that the advice is from a *trustworthy*, ideally independent source. For example, there are lots of websites purporting to "review" anonymizing services when really these websites are not quite as unbiased as they claim. Too often, these sites are acting unethically and posing as independent reviewers in an attempt to lure you into signing up for services that generate commissions. Ethical practice dictates that reviewers should disclose when they are serving up potentially commission-generating affiliate links.

Similarly, take any speed ratings you find with a grain of salt as a service's download speed will vary for a number of reasons, including how geographically close the service's servers and exit gateways are located to you as well as to the other peers in the swarm, the amount of "load" (the number of total users at any one time), the number of servers, the quality of the connection, which ISP you use, and many more. For example, one person's experience with the speed of a service could be very good, while another person's experience is much less satisfactory. The best way to determine if the service's speed is good for you is to sign up for a trial or a short timeframe and test it thoroughly.

Privacy Policy
One of the most, if not *the* most, important things to confirm is that the service offers very strong privacy protections for its customers. As boring as it may sound, read the legalese on their website, whether it is called a Privacy Policy, Terms of Service or Legal Information. What you are looking for here are elements of strong privacy protections extended to customers (you).

For example, do they keep logs? Do they disclose user information? If so, under what circumstances? If these answers are not readily apparent, then write to them to find out.

Top Tip - If you want to contact the service and remain anonymous when doing so, communicate with them using a disposable email address – see the resources at http://www.cogipas.com/disposable-email/.

In order to ensure your maximum privacy, choose a torrent anonymizing service that does not keep any logs. This way, even if they have to disclose information, for example pursuant to a court order or the direction of a state authority, there is nothing meaningful for the anonymizing service to actually disclose as it doesn't keep any logs of user activity.

Even after you select and sign up for a torrent anonymizing service, keep an eye on their privacy policy (by whatever name it goes by). An easy way to do this is to place an alert for the page using a service like ChangeDetection (free) at http://www.changedetection.com/. This way, any time the terms materially change, you will receive a notification by email alerting you about it. This is important because your VPN is unlikely to highlight when it *weakens* its privacy policy. When a service reduces the protections afforded by its privacy policy you can expect them instead to make the change as quietly as possible without alerting customers.

Recommended Torrent Anonymizing Services

If you want to skip doing the research yourself, I provide some recommended torrent anonymizing services in this section. Or maybe you did your homework and arrived at the same conclusions as I did. Either way, I can recommend the torrent anonymizing services below.

I have personally used these torrent anonymizing services. I am comfortable recommending them to you based on my own personal satisfaction with the factors I believe are most important, including:

→ Privacy (strong customer protections regarding logging)

→ Reliability (minimal downtime and connection drops)

→ Speed (fast downloading)

→ Ease of use (installation, setup and day-to-day use)

→ Breadth (lots of different exit gateway locations)

Of course, each service is different and has its own particular features. In the end, the choice is yours. You can choose to select one of the services I recommend or do your own research. Always remember, the performance of a particular service will depend on a number of things (I went over them briefly a few pages back) so do some homework before signing up to *any* service.

For full transparency, please note that some of my recommendations contain affiliate links (indicated by a cents sign, ¢). I would never promote services that I don't personally believe in as that would undermine the hard work I put into my books and all of my related efforts. And remember, if you do click on these ¢ links and ultimately sign up, it doesn't cost you anything extra as it is the vendor, not you, who absorbs the cost of the commissions.

Private Internet Access

Private Internet Access or PIA (premium ¢) via http://www.cogipas.com/pia gets very high marks on the five factors above. After signing up and paying for the service, you will receive your *userid* and *password* credentials by email and be asked to download their app depending on the kind of device(s) you have. After installing the app, you enter your credentials and off you go! The app lets you choose the exit gateway locations or you can simply rely on the "auto" feature to make the choices for you.

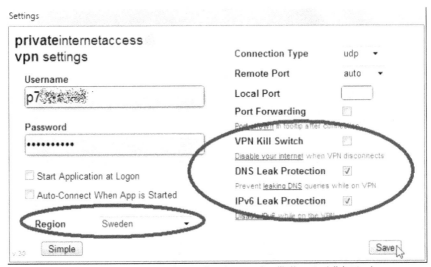

Figure 2: PIA's app supports region selection and a "kill switch" (Windows app shown)

PIA also supports advanced features like a "kill switch" and leak protection. On my wish list for PIA would be that its app display a little more detail. Currently, only a small green icon indicates you are connected and I wish I could see more details about the connection, masked IP address and speed when the service is enabled.

Top Tip - A *kill switch* means that your Internet connection is disabled should your connection to the anonymizing VPN service unexpectedly disconnect. This helps ensure that your true IP address is not compromised. *Leak protection* ensures that some special connections your device makes at a very low technical level are also routed through the VPN, enabling the maximum level of privacy and security possible.

To get a feel for the service before purchasing it, see their installation and FAQ pages, https://www.privateinternetaccess.com/pages/client-support/ (once you select your operating system, just cancel the automatic download that tries to start).

Supports: Windows, Mac OS, Linux, iOS, Android

Tech Specs: PPTP, OpenVPN, L2TP IPSec, SOCKS5

Exit gateway locations: US | US, Canada, UK, Switzerland, Netherlands, Sweden, France, Germany, Romania, Hong Kong

Privacy: PIA cannot match specific users to any activity on their service because they do not keep traffic logs and they use shared IP address technology. See PIA's full privacy policy here, https://www.privateinternetaccess.com/pages/privacy-policy/.

Price: **special reader offers** of $5.95 monthly or $36.95 annually ($3.08/mo.) via http://www.cogipas.com/pia | normal price $6.95 monthly or $39.95 annually ($3.33/mo.)

Payment methods: PayPal, VISA, Mastercard, AMEX, Discover, Google Checkout, Amazon Payment, BitCoin, Liberty Reserve, OK Pay, CashU

PureVPN

PureVPN (premium ¢) via http://www.cogipas.com/purevpn is a service that I have been using for more than a year and I have only praise for them.

Established in 2006, PureVPN has been around for a while and is super easy to use. After opening an account on the PureVPN website you will receive a confirmation email with your *userid* and *password* for accessing the service. This same email will also contain links to their apps for each type of supported device (Windows/Mac OS/Linux/iOS/Android). After installing their app and entering your userid and password, you will be anonymously downloading torrents in no time (pictured below). That's all there is to it.

Figure 3: PureVPN.com's easy-to-use anonymizing app (Windows app shown)

In addition to excelling in all of the five factors listed at the start of this section, I just really like using PureVPN's app. In one easy place, I can *Quick Connect* relying on the service to choose the best options for me or I can opt for *Personalized Selection* choosing how and through which exit gateways to connect. The *Dashboard* lets me see my connection speed at a glance. PureVPN encrypts my traffic and anonymizes my IP address.

PureVPN's speed and reliability have been consistently excellent over the entire time that I have been a customer. Perhaps it's purely psychological, but I also derive some comfort from them being headquartered outside of the US and the EU. I also like PureVPN's *Split Tunneling* feature which lets me cherry-pick which apps' Internet traffic to route through the service. My only wish list item for PureVPN would be a "kill switch" (see the previous *Top Tip*), but I'm told that it's coming soon.

To get a feel for PureVPN before you try or buy it, see their tutorial pages at http://www.purevpn.com/tutorials.php.

PureVPN is affordable, reliable and backed up by good 24/7 online live chat support staffed by actual human beings– no endless death loops of reading generic FAQs. I use PureVPN primarily for anonymously downloading torrents, but as it is a full-fledged VPN that protects my entire Internet connection, I also use it as a web anonymizing service for web browsing.

Supports: Windows, Mac OS, Linux, iOS, Android

Tech Specs: PPTP, L2TP IPSec, SSTP

HQ | Exit gateway locations: Hong Kong | US, UK, Australia, Brazil, Canada, Costa Rica, Egypt, France, Germany*, Ireland, Latvia, Luxembourg*, Malaysia, Netherlands*, Panama, Romania*, Russia*, Singapore, Sweden*, Switzerland, Turkey* (*denotes torrent-friendly gateways)

Privacy: PureVPN does not store actual VPN service usage logs, nor does it store user's personal data to share with anyone. Since PureVPN does not store user activity logs, its users are assured of full anonymity and security. See PureVPN's full privacy policy here, http://www.purevpn.com/privacy-policy.php.

Price: check for ***special reader offers*** via
http://www.cogipas.com/purevpn | normal price $11.95 monthly | 3-day money back guarantee

Payment methods: PayPal, VISA, Mastercard, AMEX, Discover, BitCoin, MoneyBookers, AlertPay, WebMoney, Western Union, bank transfer

Whether you choose one of my recommended torrent anonymizing services or find one on your own, you are now ready to download torrents anonymously. The steps that follow will show you how.

PART II – HOW TO DOWNLOAD TORRENTS ANONYMOUSLY IN STEP-BY-STEP DETAILS

Introduction

The sections below explain in detail the steps you need to take to download torrents as privately and anonymously as possible. I highly recommend that you use *both* an IP address protection tool (step 1) and a torrent anonymizing service (step 2) when downloading and sharing torrents. However, if you make the informed choice *not* to use one or both of them, you can skip these steps and still enjoy torrents. But please understand that you will be compromising your privacy and will *not* be anonymous (your IP address will be easily ascertained by the snoops I mentioned in Part I). That may be fine for some people provided that they understand the trade-offs they are making.

As mentioned, the screenshots below are for my current "go to" torrent app, µTorrent, and anonymizing service, PureVPN, on a Windows device. If you use a different torrent app, anonymizing service or device, your screens may look different, perhaps substantially different, but the same general concepts will apply almost universally.

Step 1: Start your IP Address Protection Tool

I recommend that you use a tool that blocks undesirable or otherwise "unfriendly" IP addresses from connecting to your devices. As mentioned in Part I, the tool I currently use and recommend is PeerBlock (free) at http://www.peerblock.com/. PeerBlock acts similar to firewall software, but goes one step further as it filters the IP addresses trying to connect to your devices against specialized "blacklists" compiled by passionate torrent enthusiasts.

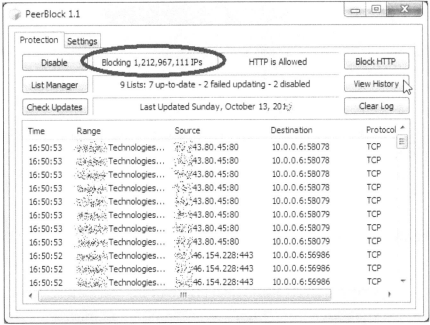

Figure 4: I'm being protected from over 1 billion potentially unfriendly IP addresses (PeerBlock shown)

The "blacklist" filters that PeerBlock lets you choose from include those protecting you from IP addresses associated with snoopers, spammers, spyware, educational institutions, governments and, of course, anti-torrent elements (called *Anti-P2P* in the lists). The anti-p2p lists are especially handy as they block the IP addresses of some organizations believed to be monitoring the torrents people are downloading. In addition, you can easily add even more custom blacklists (some free, some premium) from resources such as http://iblocklist.com/lists.php.

You will be taken through a setup wizard the first time you run PeerBlock. In addition to the list called Anti-P2P, select any other lists of interest to you. Also choose how frequently you want the lists to be updated; I recommend daily.

Top Tip - PeerBlock provides particularly useful protection when downloading torrents, but you can also use it for *all* your Internet activities, including web browsing. If PeerBlock is blocking access to a website, app or service that you do wish to access, it is easy with a simple right-click to grant access, whether for 15 minutes, an hour or permanently.

Mac users will need to rely on the similar built-in feature found in the torrent app, Transmission. From Transmission's menu, make the following choices: Preferences > Peers > under the Blocklist section check beside "Prevent Known Bad Peers from Connecting". While you are at it, update the list and select Automatically Update.

In other words, an IP protection tool is the *first* layer of armor in protecting your privacy, whether or not you use a torrent anonymizing service (discussed next).

Step 2: Start your Torrent Anonymizing Service
Whichever torrent anonymizing service you decide to use, launch it before you start downloading or sharing any torrents.

If your torrent anonymizing service supports advanced privacy settings, use them. For example, the screenshot below shows me using PureVPN's advanced features, always (1) selecting 'Higher Security and anonymity' (as opposed to just wanting to circumvent geographic restrictions for streaming video or music online) and (2) choosing exit gateways that are located outside of the US and EU before (3) connecting. When you ever want to disconnect from the service, this is easily done at the click of a button.

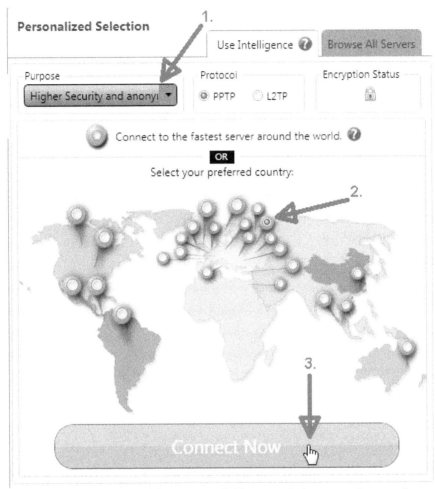

Figure 5: Use any advanced features available to maximize your privacy and anonymity

Once connected, take note of your masked IP address as you will need it for the next step. By masked IP address I mean the IP address that your torrent anonymizing service assigned to you for this session. It should be easy for you to determine. For example, with PureVPN, the IP address assigned to you at any given time can be seen in the upper-right hand corner of their app.

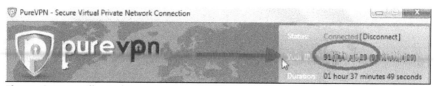

Figure 6: You will need to note down your masked IP address for the next step

To determine your IP address if using Private Internet Access, visit their handy 'What's My IP' page at https://www.privateinternetaccess.com/pages/whats-my-ip/. Although this page displays your IP address for web browsing (http/https), as PIA is a full-fledged VPN protecting your entire Internet connection, the IP address displayed on this page will also be your masked IP address for your peer-to-peer (p2p) torrent activities.

Figure 7: PIA's website has a handy page that displays your IP address

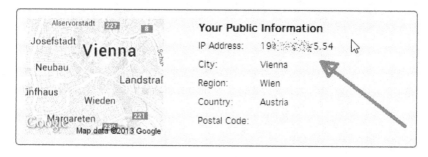

Figure 8: You will need to note down your masked IP address for the next step

Step 3: Confirm what IP Address your Torrent App is Transmitting

Now you can start your torrent app. If you haven't already installed one, see my earlier recommendations in Part I.

Before you start enthusiastically downloading or sharing torrents, you should first check what IP address your torrent app is transmitting. In other words, make sure that your anonymizing service from step 2 is functioning and masking your true IP address. This way you can be assured that snoops will not be able to ascertain, let alone monitor, your IP address and torrent downloads.

If you last closed your torrent app while it was in the midst of downloading or sharing torrents, select all of the active torrents in your torrent app and pause them for now until you finish this confirmation step. If you don't pause your active torrents and something is wrong with your anonymizing service (for example, you forgot to activate it or it is temporarily down), your true IP address could be transmitted, risking its disclosure.

Figure 9: Pause any active torrents in your torrent app (µTorrent shown)

Top Tip - It is good to get in the habit of pausing your active torrents every time *before* shutting down your torrent app. That way, the next time you start your torrent app, no torrents will be active.

To check what IP address your torrent app is transmitting, you will need to perform a *specific* method of verification. It is *useless* to visit plain old "what's my IP address" websites for checking whether your torrent anonymizing service is working. In fact, this can be a dangerous practice because it can give you a completely false sense of anonymity. Let me explain.

As mentioned, it can be the case that an anonymizing service hides your IP address when browsing the web, but not for downloading torrents. So, if you visited a "what's my IP address" website it would display your masked IP address, giving you the impression that your online presence is anonymous and encouraging you to download torrents thinking that you are protected. Unknown to you, it's only your web browsing that's being anonymized and *not* your torrent activities. Therefore, a different way of checking your transmitted IP address is needed for confirming your torrent activities are being protected.

As a reminder, *web surfing* and *torrents* use completely different protocols. Web surfing uses http/https protocols while downloading torrents uses peer-to-peer/p2p protocols. Of course, the best anonymizing services, such as VPNs, hide your IP address for both or, better yet, *all* Internet protocols, protecting all your online activities.

The best way to check what IP address your torrent app is transmitting is to visit www.CheckMyTorrentIP.com.

Checking the IP Address on the Site
Follow the instructions on the site by downloading the torrent featured on it (by clicking on the rather ominously named 'Generate Tracking Torrent' button).

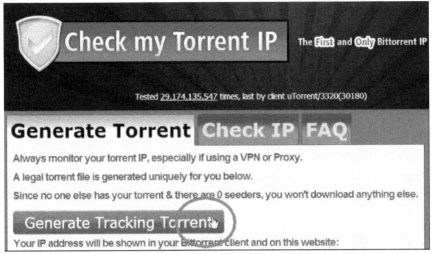

Figure 10: Download the torrent at www.CheckMyTorrentIP.com

You will be prompted to download a torrent file. Once it is downloaded, open the torrent with your torrent app just as you would normally for any other torrent. You will see that the torrent's payload is a small image file, *CheckMyTorrentIP.jpg* (see the image below).

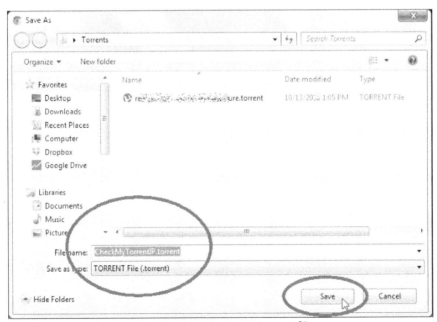

Figure 11: Downloading the *CheckMyTorrentIP.torrent* file

Your torrent app will dutifully attempt to download the image, but it will never actually succeed. But that's exactly the point. This keeps the torrent in a continual downloading mode so that the CheckMyTorrentIP service can detect and regularly report the IP address that your torrent app is transmitting. Let's check this.

You can check the IP address being transmitted by your torrent app in two ways, 1) checking on the same website and/or 2) checking the trackers in your torrent app.

On the same CheckMyTorrentIP website, go to the second tab 'Check IP'. This page will display the IP address that is trying to download the torrent you just grabbed. As that torrent was uniquely generated only for you, the IP address shown corresponds to the one transmitted by your torrent app. Helpfully, the page also displays the country associated with your IP address.

Figure 12: Checking your IP address on the CheckMyTorrentIP website

This IP address should *not* be your true IP address, but instead the IP address assigned by your torrent anonymizing service. If it displays your *true* IP address, something is wrong. Either the torrent anonymizing service is not functioning (double-check that you actually did activate it in Step 2) or it does not work with torrents, the peer-to-peer/p2p protocol. If it displays your masked IP address, then you know that your torrent anonymizing service is working.

For a video recap of this process, see http://www.cogipas.com/CMTIP-recap.

Checking the Trackers in your Torrent App

You can also perform this verification check from within your torrent app. This might provide you with some additional comfort if you are paranoid or skeptical since checking in this way is independent from the CheckMyTorrentIP website.

In your torrent app's list of torrents, select the torrent you just downloaded and check its *Trackers*. In μTorrent, trackers can be found displayed under the tab *Trackers* (at box 2 in the screenshot below).

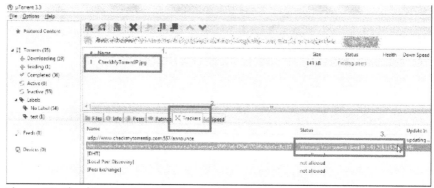

Figure 13: Checking the *Trackers* for the CheckMyTorrentIP torrent in your app (μTorrent shown)

You will see (in lower right-hand highlighted area of the screenshot above) that a Warning error is displayed (don't worry) but also a short message right after it reporting on the IP address that your torrent app is transmitting. Check it carefully. This IP address should *not* be your true IP address, but instead be the IP address assigned by your torrent anonymizing service.

If the warning displayed under the Tracking tab displays your *true* IP address rather than your masked one, something is wrong. Either the torrent anonymizing service is not functioning (double-check that you did actually activate it in Step 2) or it does not work with torrents, the peer-to-peer/p2p protocol. Of course, the torrent anonymizing services I recommend work with all Internet protocols, including p2p. If the Trackers for the CheckMyTorrentIP torrent report your masked IP address, you know that your torrent anonymizing service is working.

Regardless of the verification method you used above, keep the CheckMyTorrentIP torrent active in your torrent app even though the payload image will never download. This way, every time you open your torrent app you can quickly check the Trackers for this torrent and, as above, confirm that your anonymizing service is working and that your true IP address remains hidden from snoops.

Top Tip - If you are using a torrent app that displays ads, you can actually use these ads to your advantage. The ads can serve as yet another verification that your torrent anonymizing service is working. If your torrent app is displaying ads from the location of your torrent anonymizing service's exit gateways rather than the location of your true IP address, this gives you further comfort that the service is working.

Once you confirm your torrent anonymizing service is working, you can confidently go about downloading and sharing torrents (you can also now safely un-pause any torrents that were already loaded).

Step 4: Use a Web Anonymizing Service When Visiting Websites Related to Your Torrents

I know you are keen to start finding and downloading torrents, but there is an often overlooked interim step that I need to tell you about. As a further precaution, you should visit any websites related to your torrent activities with a *web* anonymizing service enabled. This means enabling your web anonymizing service (whether a premium service or a free one like TOR or Hotspot Shield, or a full-fledged VPN) when visiting websites like torrent-related forums, movie subtitle archives, torrent indexing sites (these "torrent search engines" are discussed next at step 5), and perhaps even the CheckMyTorrentIP website from step 3 above. There is little sense taking the precautions outlined in this Guide for downloading torrents anonymously only to inadvertently reveal your true IP address while searching for torrents or torrent-related information.

Take a simple example. You search for torrents about a private or delicate personal matter. Maybe you are looking for documents or videos about how to declare personal bankruptcy or deal with a life-threatening illness or a medical condition. Unfortunately, you conducted these searches on the web (perhaps using a major search engine) *without* taking the precaution of enabling a *web* anonymizing service (shame on you as I told you earlier about some free ones!). Those web searches are now "stamped" with your true IP address for any snoops to discover and use. Maybe the snoops are monitoring and logging the IP address information to eavesdrop on you in real-time or maybe they are collecting this information to use it later, maybe even much later.

Thirty seconds after you performed those web searches, someone with a different IP address and who seemingly lives half-way across the globe starts downloading one or more of these torrents. Of course, that person is you but you are downloading the torrents with your torrent anonymizing service enabled which transmits an entirely different IP address. But, depending on how popular those torrents are, snoops can cross reference these two separate activities - the web searches and the torrent downloads - and still pinpoint or deduce that you are the same person.

It is very simple: X searched for Y, then Z started downloading Y, therefore X must be Z.

Even for popular torrents that are being searched for and downloaded by thousands of people, don't think that you can hide in the swarms and avoid these cross-referencing techniques (called *traffic analysis*). In these more complicated cases, the conclusion to the formula above simply becomes: therefore X is more likely to be Z. But with enough cross references, this can be very accurate and the *probability* that X is Z can become almost a certainty.

Back to our simple examples, the snoops now know that you are facing personal bankruptcy or have a life-threatening medical condition. Who knows how the snoops will use this information. Perhaps you will "only" start seeing more online ads on these topics. Or maybe this information is quietly added to your profile in secret databases and later used (unknown to you) to deny you medical or insurance coverage, fail a job screening, reject a loan application, etc. Or maybe the snoops are of a criminal variety and use this sensitive personal information against you in ways ranging from harassment to extortion (don't roll your eyes, this happens, and is on the rise).

So, hopefully I have convinced you that, when engaging in any web browsing that is related to your torrent downloading activities, you should do so with a web anonymizing service enabled. You don't want to make it any easier for the snoops by downloading torrents anonymously only to then give yourself away when web browsing naked. In fact, you should use a web anonymizing service for all of your sensitive web browsing, but especially regarding your torrents.

Step 5: Find Torrents to Download and Share (Torrent Indexes and Searching Tips)

To find torrents, it is better to use reliable *torrent indexing sites* than general Internet search engines. This is because torrent indexing sites are essentially search engines specializing in torrents and usually only torrents, whereas search engines, especially the market leaders, are trying to cater to everyone's search needs. And, anyway, some of the major search engines seem to be increasingly censoring torrent search results, primarily due to copyright concerns.

The best torrent indexing site(s) for you to use may depend on the *type* of payload items you are looking for, whether movies, music, apps, video clips, games, books, erotica, images, etc.

Torrent indexing sites are usually searchable *and* browseable. This means that you can search for torrents by keywords (just like any search engine you are used to), but also explore a structured set of categories which are sometimes further divided into sub-categories.

In particular, community-based torrent indexing sites offer a number of additional advantages. Members of these communities post comments and sometimes assign ratings for torrents which can help screen out poor quality, copyright, fake or malware-infected items.

Most torrent indexes will also display the number of seeders and leechers for each torrent. Usually, they just use the term "seeds" for seeders and "peers" for leechers (even if technically a seed is also a peer). Usually, the greater number of seeds and peers you see, the more popular the torrent.

How to Tell which Torrents will Download Fastest

Torrents download fastest the higher the ratio of seeds to peers (the greater percentage of seeds in a swarm, the faster you can expect to download the torrent). In other words, if torrent X has 100 seeds and 200 peers, while torrent Y has 10 seeds and 10 peers, you could expect torrent Y to download faster even though its swarm is smaller in size and has fewer total participants. That's because the percentage (ratio) of seeds to peers for torrent Y is 100% whereas for torrent X it is 50%. Size isn't everything, the *ratio* is what's more important.

Copyright-Safe Torrent Indexes

Copyright safety is also a factor in determining which torrent indexing sites to visit because, unfortunately, too often the most popular torrent indexing sites include torrents associated with pirated materials.

Good starting points for copyright-safe torrent indexing sites that should be clear of torrents associated with pirated materials include:

➔ **Mininova** at http://www.mininova.org/ - an easy-to-use directory and search engine for all kinds of torrent files.

➔ **ClearBits** at http://www.clearbits.net/ - a torrent directory of open licensed media, including movies, music, games and more.

➔ **BitTorrent's Featured Content** at http://bundles.bittorrent.com/ - torrents featured by the firm that invented them (it's in their interest to offer exciting legal torrents).

➔ **Internet Archive** at http://archive.org/details/bittorrent - movies, music and books that are now in the public domain (lots of "classics" from the past).

➔ **VODO** at http://vodo.net/ - torrents of independent ("indie") film and movies.

➔ **Vuze Wiki** at http://wiki.vuze.com/w/Legal_torrent_sites maintains a great list of legal torrent sites, organized by category.

Copyright-friendly torrent indexes can also be found using a general Internet search engine and typing terms like "legal torrent indexing sites" or "best legal torrents".

Popular Torrent Indexes

Lists of the most popular torrent indexing sites (as measured by the number of monthly visitors) can be found here:

➔ http://torrentfreak.com/top-10-most-popular-torrent-sites-of-2013-130106/

➔ http://www.ebizmba.com/articles/torrent-websites

Popular torrent indexing sites can also be found using a general Internet search engine and typing terms like "most popular torrent indexing sites", "torrent search engine" or even simply "torrents". However, remember what I said earlier about copyright safety. In addition, some of the most popular torrent index sites have very cluttered pages, trying to entice you into clicking on all kinds of ads, downloads and other links, not all of which might be safe or desirable.

Top Tip - Although Google is the most popular search engine, try using different search engines like Bing at http://www.bing.com/ as you may get different results. In addition, consider using alternative search engines that better respect your privacy and don't track you, such as DuckDuckGo at https://duckduckgo.com/ and Ixquick at https://www.ixquick.com/.

You could also include terms matching the category or type of payload items you are looking for, whether movies, music, apps, video clips, games, books, erotica, images, etc. For even more specific searches you could also include any subcategory that is of specific interest. For example,

➔ torrent search engine documentary movies

General Search Engines

Although they provide less relevant results, you can also search *directly* for specific torrents using general Internet search engines. Searching for specific torrents directly through general search engines can occasionally unearth a hidden gem of a torrent or lead you to discover a new favorite torrent indexing site.

For general Internet search engines, you have two strategies:

You can perform a simple search for the content you seek by adding the word "torrent"

➔ documentary torrent

Or, if you know what an operator is (it's a search parameter), you can employ the *filetype:* operator on general search engines that support it. General search engines supporting this operator include Google, Bing, DuckDuckGo and Ixquick.

Here is an example of a torrent search on a general search engine using the *filetype:* operator.

➜   documentary filetype:torrent

Top Tip - Note that there is *no space* between the colon (:) and the word torrent. Also note that it's torrent singular, not torrents plural.

Step 6: Start Downloading and Sharing Torrents!
Of all the steps, this is the easiest and most fun.

Use your torrent app just like I showed you earlier. Of course, the difference now is that your IP address protection tool will be shielding your device and your torrent anonymizing service will be masking your true IP address.

When you find torrents that you want to download, save them to your device and open them in your torrent app. The screenshot below shows me selecting a torrent file to download (using the Chrome web browser).

Figure 14: Downloading a torrent file on the web is like downloading any other item, just click on it

Upon clicking on the link, the web browser prompts me to download the torrent file.

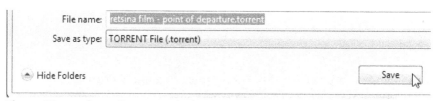

Figure 15: ...and save it on your device

Remember that torrent files themselves usually download in a matter of seconds because they are just small text files. Once downloaded, click on the torrent and it will open in your torrent app. Depending on the torrent app you are using, select which payload items you want to download (usually all the payload items are selected by default) and where on your device you want to save them, and click OK to start downloading.

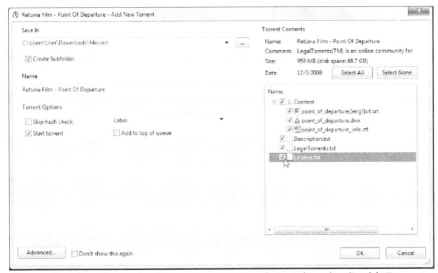

Figure 16: Select the payload items you want and start downloading! (µTorrent shown)

Now you can watch with glee as your torrent app tries to negotiate with the swarm and start downloading the torrent's payload. As mentioned, sometimes payloads download quickly, other times less so. How fast the payload items download is mostly a function of how big a percentage of the swarm is made up of seeds for a given torrent.

When a torrent finishes downloading, it is up to you whether to let it seed or to stop sharing it. But remember, good torrent etiquette dictates that you should *share* torrents, not just download them. After all, if no one seeded, torrents would be much more difficult to download in the first place. So do your fair share of sharing!

Optional Final Steps: Encrypt Your Torrent Downloads and Wash-Up Your Device

As mentioned, both of these steps are optional and a matter of personal preference. For the small investment of time and effort (and no or little cost), I take these extra steps to further safeguard my torrent downloading habits from being discovered by anyone with, or gaining, access to my device.

Now that you are protected from the *online* snoops, ideally you should also strive to keep your torrents and downloads safe from the prying eyes of *offline* snoops. Not to sound alarmist, but there may be little sense taking precautions for downloading torrents anonymously only to inadvertently leave obvious traces of your activities on your device. Preventing this means taking one or two additional (but also easy) steps to minimize your *offline* fingerprints.

To best protect yourself, encrypt your torrent downloads and further cleanse your device of the traces of your torrent activities. These two steps are described below.

Encryption

Downloading torrents is so easy and fun, it can become addictive. Soon you will be downloading lots of torrent payloads ranging from movies, music, ebooks, images, documents, videos clips and more. However, with all these items saved on your device, it is all too easy for them to be discovered.

Now encryption is a word that may frighten off some people and conjure up all sorts of complicated concepts. But these days, encryption is very easy to use, including very strong "military grade" encryption that is virtually uncrackable to even the most determined and well-funded of potential adversaries. As a bonus, some of the leading encryption apps are free.

Encryption apps let you quickly and easily encrypt selected items or folders, entire devices, USB sticks, external hard drives and even cloud-based storage solutions. With these options, you can keep your private torrents encrypted on your device, removable storage or in the cloud.

Further, the encryption process does not take up any additional storage space or time.

Enter password for C:\Users\User\Documents\xBAK\data.dat

Password:	********************	OK
Cache passwords and keyfiles in memory		Cancel
Display password		
Use keyfiles	Keyfiles...	Mount Options...

Figure 17: After entering your password, presto, the previously invisible encrypted items will instantly appear

Again, think of encryption like having the combination to an impenetrable safe that only you can open. Once you have encrypted your torrents, accessing them only takes a matter of seconds after entering the correct passphrase of your choosing. After each torrent downloading session, simply re-encrypt the location at a single click and everything will be safely hidden among billions of random bytes of data that can only be accessed with your password. To anyone that does not possess the correct password you established, the unencrypted data, whether on your device, separate storage media or in the cloud, will merely appear as a random jumble of data. Nothing to see here folks, just move along.

Encryption really couldn't be any easier and *everyone* should now be using it, especially for their torrents.

Top Tip - An encryption app password is completely different from the password that, for example, Windows may ask you for. Even if a casual snoop or determined adversary doesn't know your Windows password, they can *easily* access all of the (non-encrypted) data on your computer using a number of methods. For example, they could startup your computer from a "live CD" to gain complete access to everything on it. A live CD is a CD, DVD or USB thumb drive containing an alternative operating system used to "boot" your computer. Examples include Puppy Linux or the Tails live operating system. Once inside your system, the snoops can view and copy any data without you even knowing about it.

It's never fun having your private material discovered, whether accidentally by someone innocently coming across it or intentionally by someone looking to gain advantage over you. Even if you don't share your device with anyone, it may be that someone is actively looking for these items in an attempt to harm you. As mentioned, there are plenty of stories where someone's private material has been used against them by determined adversaries ranging from exes, private investigators, divorce attorneys, rogue co-workers, business rivals, nosy neighbors, trolls, hackers, or even Big Brother.

Or maybe you are even craftier and keep your stash on a separate storage device like an external hard drive or USB stick. For sure that is safer and a magnitude better at protecting your private material, but hardly fool-proof. Storing data in the cloud (for example, via services like Dropbox or Google Drive) comes with similar risks.

Saving your private material on portable storage or in the cloud is a fine system as long as it remains a secret. But if someone comes across the storage media or sees you interacting with a cloud storage service they may ask "what's that?" Worse, if they don't believe you or you are not around, they may plug in the media or start poking around your device's cloud-synched folders and items, especially if you remain logged in or have auto-logon features enabled.

One caveat here: you can use encryption to hide your private torrents and payload items, but some offline traces of your activities will still remain on your device (unless you are encrypting your entire device as opposed to certain folders or items on it). These sources of trace data include hidden records kept and left behind by your device's system, browser and other apps, such as movie players, image viewers, document readers, music players etc. So, after downloading and encrypting your torrents, you should still use a washing-up app as your last step (discussed next).

Top Tip - You should consider *fully* encrypting your devices in this way if for no other reason than to protect your data in the event of theft. For example, identity thieves could have a field day with all of the personal materials on your unencrypted device. However, if the same device were encrypted, they would have stolen only a very expensive doorstop or paperweight. The device may remain stolen (a major bummer) but at least your data will be safe and you will be spared the worst kind of nightmare.

As a final note, of course it is vital that you use super strong passwords for encrypting. Do *not* use passwords that are easily crackable and leave you vulnerable. At a minimum, this means using long passwords (pass*phrases* is a more accurate term) that are a mix of letters, uppercase and lowercase, as well as numbers and symbols.

Better yet, use a password management app like LastPass (free) at https://lastpass.com/ for Windows, Mac OS, Linux, iOS and Android to help you generate and keep track of super strong passwords for apps (and websites too).

Washing-Up

After anonymously downloading torrents and their payloads, protecting them with encryption and closing your apps, the last step is to eliminate any remaining traces of torrent activities from your device. After each torrent downloading session, use a washing-up app to eliminate these offline digital fingerprints for good.

If using a washing-up app strikes you as a step too much, that's fine as it is completely optional. But again, there are some good apps available, including free ones, so why not do everything you can to protect your torrent activities from disclosure offline as well as online. I provided some recommended apps in Part I.

Typically, these apps let you select which features of your operating system and apps to cleanse (see Figure 18). Good selections include your trash or recycle bin, temporary files (sometimes called cache items), and lists of recent activity kept by your device's operating system and its apps, including those you use to enjoy your downloaded torrent payloads.

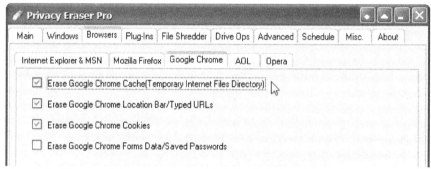

Figure 18: Most washing-up apps provide lots of choice about what you can cleanse from your device

A Final Word

Congratulations! You've made it through many pages of not always easy information.

The good news is that you now have all the knowledge you need to protect your privacy and download torrents anonymously. Although there are real risks when downloading torrents, you should try not to be paranoid about them. Don't forget to *have fun* too.

Happy torrenting!

* * *

I hope that you enjoyed this Guide. I put a lot of hard work into it and I am very proud of the end result. Please consider providing a review. Even just assigning a star-rating and adding a few words would be greatly appreciated as this gives me valuable feedback. Thanks!

➜ to leave a review on **Amazon USA**, please visit via
http://www.cogipas.com/Amazon-USA

➜ to leave a review on **Amazon UK**, please visit via
http://www.cogipas.com/Amazon-UK

➜ to leave a review on any **other** site, please visit via
http://www.cogipas.com/the-books/

Annex: Quick Start Resources

Summarized below in one handy list are the apps and services recommended in this Guide for anonymously downloading and sharing torrents.

For full transparency, please note that some of the following recommendations contain affiliate links (indicated by a cents sign, ¢). I would never promote services that I don't personally believe in as that would undermine the hard work I put into my books and all of my related efforts. And remember, if you do click on these links and ultimately sign up, it doesn't cost you anything extra as it is the vendor, not you, who absorbs the cost of the commissions.

Torrent Apps

µTorrent (free) at http://www.utorrent.com/ for Windows and Mac OS.

µTorrent (free) via http://goo.gl/41X1lg or http://www.utorrent.com/utorrent-android for Android.

Vuze (free) at http://www.vuze.com/ for Windows, Mac OS and Linux.

Transmission (free) at http://www.transmissionbt.com/ for Mac OS.

IP Address Protection Tools

PeerBlock (free) at http://www.peerblock.com/ for Windows. More "blacklists" for use with PeerBlock can be obtained from **I-BlockList** (most free) at http://www.iblocklist.com/.

Mac users will have to rely on the IP protection features built into the torrent app above, *Transmission*.

Torrent Anonymizing Services

PureVPN (premium ¢) via http://www.cogipas.com/purevpn (check for *special reader offers*) for Windows, Mac OS, Linux, iOS and Android - a full-fledged VPN service anonymizing all of your Internet traffic including torrents and web browsing.

Private Internet Access or **PIA** (premium ¢) via http://www.cogipas.com/pia (with *special reader offers*) for Windows, Mac OS, Linux, iOS and Android - a full-fledged VPN service anonymizing all of your Internet traffic including torrents and web browsing.

Web Anonymizing Services

TOR Project (free) at https://www.torproject.org/ for Windows, Mac OS and Linux —suitable as an anonymizing service for web browsing, *not* torrenting.

HotspotShield (free) at http://www.hotspotshield.com/ for Windows, Mac OS, iOS and Android —suitable as an anonymizing service for web browsing, *not* torrenting. In exchange for being free, the service displays ads.

To anonymize your web browsing, you can also use a full-fledged VPN service like those above, **Private Internet Access** (premium ¢) via http://www.cogipas.com/pia (with *special reader offers*) and **PureVPN** (premium ¢) via http://www.cogipas.com/purevpn (check for *special reader offers*).

Encryption Apps

TrueCrypt (free) at http://www.truecrypt.org/ for Windows, Mac OS and Linux.

SSE-Universal Encryption App (free) via http://goo.gl/o6UmeO for Android.

Encryption Buddy (premium) via http://goo.gl/w3TsVa for Mac OS.

Safe (premium) via http://goo.gl/ZiDIjj for iOS.

Folder Lock (premium after free trial period) at http://www.newsoftwares.net/folderlock/ for Windows.

Password Management Apps

LastPass (free) at https://lastpass.com/ for Windows, Mac OS, Linux and iOS.

LastPass (premium) at https://lastpass.com/ for Android.

Washing-Up Apps

Privacy Eraser Pro (premium ¢) via http://www.cogipas.com/pep for Windows. It comes with a trial evaluation period, supports all major web browsers and includes access to hundreds of plug-ins available for almost every app imaginable – some that you probably didn't even know were keeping offline records of your activities. As an added bonus, it comes with a built-in file wiping utility for permanently deleting items on your device (acting like an electronic shredder).

CCleaner (free) at http://www.piriform.com/ccleaner for Windows and Mac OS, supporting all major web browser apps.

Clean Master (free) via http://goo.gl/0rNgbX for Android.

iCleaner (premium) via http://goo.gl/y6q5UF for iOS.

Further Reading

Complete Guide to Internet Privacy, Anonymity & Security (premium ¢) via http://www.cogipas.com/the-books/ – my first book available in Kindle and hardcopy (Windows focus).

Take Control of Your Online Privacy (premium ¢) via http://www.cogipas.com/tcop (more Mac focused).

For updates and more resources, please visit www.cogipas.com.

[you have reached the end of the book, that's all folks! THE END]